NO 21 '02	DATE DUE		

Rare and Interesting Stamps

by

Cindy Dyson

Chelsea House Publishers
Philadelphia

CHELSEA HOUSE PUBLISHERS

Editor-in-Chief Stephen Reginald
Managing Editor James D. Gallagher
Production Manager Pamela Loos
Art Director Sara Davis
Picture Editor Judy Hasday
Senior Production Editor Lisa Chippendale
Designer Takeshi Takahashi

First Printing

1 3 5 7 9 8 6 4 2

Library of Congress Cataloging-in-Publication Data

Dyson, Cindy.
Rare and interesting stamps / by Cindy Dyson.

    p. cm. — (Costume, tradition, and culture: reflecting on
the past)
Includes bibliographical references and index.
Summary: Presents more than twenty-five stamps from different countries, including Belgium, Nicaragua, and the Virgin Islands, and discusses how they celebrate the customs,
legends, and history of their countries.

ISBN 0–7910–5171–4 (hardcover)
1. Postage stamps—Juvenile literature. [1. Postage stamps.]
I. Title. II. Series.
HE6182.D94 1998   98–35981
769.56—dc21   CIP
                                            AC

CONTENTS

INTRODUCTION

For as long as people have known that other cultures existed, they have been curious about the differences in their customs and traditions. Julius Caesar, the famous Roman leader, wrote long chronicles about the inhabitants of Gaul (modern-day France) while he was leading troops in the Gallic Wars (58–51 B.C.). In the chronicles, he discussed their religious beliefs, their customs, their day-to-day life, and the conflicts among the different groups. Explorers like Marco Polo traveled thousands of miles and devoted years of their lives to learning about the peoples of the East and bringing home the stories of Chinese court life, along with the silks, spices, and inventions of that culture. The Chelsea House series *Costume, Tradition, and Culture: Reflecting on the Past* continues this legacy of exploration and discovery by discussing some of the most fascinating traditions, beliefs, legends, and artifacts from around the world.

Different cultures develop traditions and costumes to mark the roles of people in their societies, to commemorate events in their histories, and to make the changes and mysteries of life more meaningful. Soldiers wear uniforms to show that they are serving in their nation's army, and insignia on the uniforms show what ranks they hold within the army. People of Bukhara, a city in Uzbekistan, have for centuries woven fine threads of gold into their clothes, and when they travel to other cities they can be recognized as Bukharans by the golden embroidery on their traditional costume. For many years, in the Irish countryside, people would leave bowls of milk outside at night as an offering to the fairies, or "Good People," believing that this would help ensure their favor and keep the family safe from fairy mischief. In Mexico, November 2 is the Day of the Dead, when people visit cemeteries and have feasts to remember their ancestors. In the United States, brides wear white dresses, and the traditional wedding includes many rituals: the father of the bride "giving her away" to the groom, the exchange of vows and rings, the throwing of rice, the tossing of the bride's bouquet. These rituals and symbols help make the marriage meaningful and special for the couple, their families, and their friends, by expressing the change that is taking place and allowing the friends and families to wish luck to the couple.

This series will explore some of the myths, symbols, costumes, and traditions of various cultures from around the world and different times in the past. *Fighting Units of the American War of Independence,* for example, will detail the uniforms, weapons, and decorations of the regiments and battalions on both sides of the war, along with the battles in which they became famous. *Roman Myths, Heroes, and Legends* describes how the ancient Romans explained the wonders and natural phenomena of their world with fantastic stories of superhuman heroes and almost human deities who could change the course of history at will. In *Popular Superstitions,* you will learn how some familiar superstitious beliefs—such as throwing spilled salt over your shoulder, or hanging a horseshoe over your door for good luck—originally began, in times when people feared that devils and evil spirits were meddling in their lives. Few people still believe in malicious spirits, but many still toss the spilled salt over their shoulders, or knock on wood when expressing cautious hope. The legendary figures of a culture—the brave explorers of *The Wild West* or the wicked brigands described in *Infamous Pirates*—help shape that culture's values by providing grand, almost mythical examples of what people should (or should not!) strive to be.

The illustrations that accompany these books have their own cultural history. Originally, they were printed on small collectors' cards and sold in the early 20th century. Each card in a set of 25 or 50 would depict a different person, artifact, or event, and usually the reverse side would offer a few sentences of description to explain the picture. Now, they provide a fascinating glimpse into history and an entertaining addition to the stories presented here.

ABOUT THE AUTHOR

CINDY DYSON is a former newspaper journalist who is now a full-time freelance writer. Her work has appeared in many national and regional magazines. This is her first book. As a teen, she enjoyed collecting stamps herself, focusing on stamps from India.

Rare and Interesting Stamps

Discovering stamps means discovering the world. Stamps introduce faraway countries with unfamiliar customs to explore, new animals to see, and unknown people to meet. A spaceship blasts away from Earth. The ancient Olympic Games of Greece are replayed, and scientists find cures to deadly diseases. All on small squares of paper.

In the more than 150 years since the first modern stamp, these tiny messengers have become more than an efficient way to get a letter from one place to another. They remind people of the tragedies and triumphs that make up world history and the people who have led countries into wars and toward peace.

Inside their tiny frames, stamps carry an impressive amount of information that lets a letter leave a hometown, skip across the United States, alight in one European country then another to eventually reach a pen pal deep in Mongolia.

The first stamp collectors, who didn't have albums but decorated walls, chairs, and tables with their stamps, would be surprised by today's philately, or stamp collecting. People have been killed for stamps. They have spent fortunes and betrayed friends for stamps. Millionaires and grammar school children with small allowances collect stamps. Some collect as an investment. Others want fame or notoriety, and some simply want to learn.

Stamps come in two types: commemorative and definitive. Commemorative stamps are printed in limited runs and celebrate some event or person or attempt to raise money. Definitive stamps are printed over and over again with the same design being used for decades.

BELGIUM: NOT ON SUNDAY

ostal officials in Belgium understood the importance of their job. If an urgent letter had to be delivered, these dedicated postal workers were willing to do the job any day of the week—even on Sundays. But like many people in this predominately Christian country, they preferred to keep the Sabbath by avoiding any work on Sunday and to rest as God instructed.

To remain dedicated to delivering the mail while still cutting down on their Sunday work, Belgium postal officials devised a scheme to accomplish both—or at least a little of both. In 1893 they added a detachable label to each stamp. The bilingual label was printed in French and Flemish, the official Belgian language, and said, "Do not deliver on a Sunday."

If the sender of a letter wanted it to be delivered even on a Sunday, he simply ripped off the stamp's label and placed the stamp on his correspondence. But because most people didn't bother to remove the label, postal workers in this small country at the southern tip of the North Sea quickly found their Sunday workloads diminishing.

In fact, the system worked so well that every Belgium stamp included a Sunday label until the beginning of World War I in late 1914. These labeled stamps, called "Sunday stamps," are particularly interesting to collectors as examples of innovative postal system methods.

The stamps here are from the 1905–1909 series showing King Leopold II and the 1913–1914 series showing King Albert I.

BELGIUM: TRAGIC QUEEN

o one in Belgium could have guessed that the three royal children featured in a stamp issued in 1935 would be motherless just a few months later. But when the children's mother, Queen Astrid, died in a motor vehicle accident, the stamp became widely collected as part of the country's mourning.

Another stamp, this one from a photograph of the beautiful, young, and popular queen herself, was issued shortly after her death as the official mourning stamp of Belgium's constitutional monarchy. Collectors and admirers rushed to buy the stamps.

Such mourning stamps with black borders had become popular in the 1930s. Germany issued a mourning stamp in 1934 after the death of President Hindenburg. Yugoslavia issued a mourning stamp in the same year when King Alexander died.

The same stamp featuring Queen Astrid was later sold to raise money to fight tuberculosis, an often deadly disease that plagued the Belgian people at the time. Belgium would continue issuing stamps to raise money to fight deadly diseases.

In 1962, it issued stamps showing a deaf, mute, and partially blind girl learning to spell to raise money for disabled children. In 1964, Belgium issued a stamp to honor men who had worked to combat leprosy, a disease that eats away at the victim's skin and internal organs and eventually leads to death.

BOSNIA-HERZEGOVINA: ASSASSINATION

n 1908 Bosnia-Herzegovina was annexed by its northern neighbor, Austria-Hungary, and many Bosnia-Herzegovinians were not happy about the loss of sovereignty. Although they retained much of their independence, students and others who wanted more freedom began planning a revolutionary movement.

In 1914 the Archduke of Austria-Hungary came to attend military maneuvers in Bosnia-Herzegovina. These revolutionaries felt Austria had gone too far and was stepping on their country's toes. One of these students, Gavrilo Princip, an 18-year-old Bosnian Serb, decided to do something about it. Princip assassinated Archduke Franz Ferdinand and his wife, Duchess Sofia, in the capital city of Sarajevo.

The assassination touched off a declaration of war by Austria-Hungary. Soon Germany declared war on Russia, and within two months most of Europe was at war. The murder in this beleaguered country at the southern reaches of Eastern Europe began World War I, which raged for four years.

In 1917, the year before the war ended, Bosnia-Herzegovina issued three ordinary-looking stamps to commemorate Ferdinand's assassination. One shows Ferdinand alone; another with Sofia. The third stamp portrays a view of a church at Sarajevo, also built to commemorate the assassination.

The stamps were sold for more than the postage they would cover in order to pay for building the church. Because the stamps never sold well, there were plenty left over, and they are still easily available—at a cost of about 75 cents for the set.

The stamp at the right depicts Ferdinand; the one at the left shows Bey's Mosque in Sarajevo.

DOMINICAN REPUBLIC: TROUBLEMAKER

mazing as it may seem, this ordinary-looking stamp issued by the Dominican Republic almost started a war. Two countries, the Dominican Republic and Haiti, share the same island in the Caribbean. It was the island Columbus first discovered on his voyage to the New World in 1492. He named the lush island Hispaniola.

The Dominican Republic and Haiti have not always gotten along well. When in 1900 the Dominican Republic issued a series of stamps depicting a map of the island including the border between the two countries, tempers flared. The Hamilton Bank Note Company printed the stamps and, for unknown reasons, drew the border so that the Dominican Republic looked larger than it really was and Haiti looked smaller.

The 50-cent stamp in the series also switched the names of the waters around the island so that "Atlantico," or the Atlantic Ocean, appears at the top of the island rather than below as it should. The Caribbean Sea, or "Mar Caribe," appears beneath the island rather than above. Meanwhile, the two-cent stamp portrayed Haiti on the right side of the island instead of in its correct position on the left.

Haitians, of course, were angry because the stamp made their country look smaller than it was. They demanded that the Dominican Republic withdraw the stamps before trouble started. The Dominican Republic agreed, replacing the stamps with ones bearing a coat of arms. It wasn't until 1929 that they issued another stamp depicting the island, this time showing the countries in their proper proportions.

The background view shows a Haitian beach.

GERMANY: MILLIONAIRE'S STAMP

A t the close of World War I, Germany's economy was in bad shape. Because the north-central European country had been an aggressor during the war, peace negotiators decided it should pay large war reparations to several of the countries it had fought. These reparation payments, along with damaged German infrastructure and general post-war suffering, led to a dramatic economic downturn.

By 1922 inflation was running rampant. When inflation is high, money becomes less valuable. What was once a $1 candy bar costs $5 one month and $10 soon after. Toward the end of their inflationary period, German people were pushing wheelbarrows full of money just to do the shopping.

The post office had a hard time keeping up with the rapidly decreasing value of money. Before inflation hit, it had cost about three pfennig to mail a letter in Germany. Inflation boosted that to 100 marks in a short time (100 pfennig equal 1 mark). Soon the price to mail a letter rose to 100,000 marks with no end in sight.

Postage printers couldn't keep up with the increases. Between August and December of 1923, almost 100 different stamps were issued as the post office tried to stay abreast. Sometimes a letter was attached to a sheet of stamps just to pay postage.

The highest priced stamp was issued in November 1923 for 50 milliard marks—50 billion marks. By this time, Germany's attempts to slow inflation's rise had begun to work, and postal rates gradually declined.

The background view shows the Brandenburg Gate, built in 1790 in Berlin.

GREAT BRITAIN: THE FIRST

Before someone had the bright idea to use stamps to pay for transporting letters from one place to another, the postal system in Great Britain, and many other countries, was a mess. The cost of mailing a letter varied according to where it was going, and people had to master complicated fee schedules. Moreover, the recipient of the letter paid for the postage rather than the sender. Postal workers had to stop and collect for each letter, and sometimes people refused to pay.

By the 1830s the British Government knew its postal service was losing too much money. In 1837 a teacher, Sir Rowland Hill, wrote a paper that would change the entire postal system of Britain and the world.

He argued that all letters weighing under half an ounce should cost just one penny to send regardless of where they were going. Also, he said that the letter's sender should pay for the postage up front. Lastly, he came up with the idea of making the stamps sticky.

The British Parliament loved Hill's idea, and by 1840 Queen Victoria had signed his idea into law. But no one knew what a stamp should look like, so the government held a contest asking people to come up with designs.

Although there were 2,600 entries, none of them looked right. Hill, who's shown in the background, came to the rescue, designing a stamp with a portrait of Queen Victoria. On May 6, 1840, the first stamp, called the "Penny Black," was mailed. Today stamps mailed on that first day are still highly sought after.

GREAT BRITAIN: GOVERNMENT PILFERING

 eople have always tried to steal from the postal system, whether making counterfeit stamps or filching them straight out. As Great Britain learned, even government officials pilfer stamps now and then. Beginning in 1882, Parliament decided to do something about it.

Special stamps called "officials" or "departments" were created to keep track of how government departments and the royal household were using stamps. Part of the tracking would check for government employees who were taking stamps from work to use for private correspondence.

Rather than creating an entirely new stamp, the government had ordinary stamps overprinted with the name of the department they were to be used for. One of the rarest of these "officials" was the overprint for the Inland Revenue Department, or the tax department.

An ordinary stamp showing King Edward VII was overprinted with "I.R. Official." These revenue stamps were used only between 1902 and 1904, making them rare and valuable (priced from $15,000 to $22,500) today. At one time they were known as the rarest British stamp, but a 1947 find of nine additional stamps bumped the known quantity to 24 and decreased the rarity of the I.R. Official.

Although Great Britain doesn't use this method to keep track of government employees anymore, overprinting is still occasionally used in countries when there is a postal rate change. Rather than printing new stamps, existing stamps are overprinted with the new value.

The background view is of Somerset House in London, where several government departments, including the revenue department, are housed.

GUYANA: UGLY BUT VALUABLE

A 12-year-old boy named Vernon Vaughan found the first—and therefore the only—one-cent British Guiana stamp while prowling through an attic in 1872. Although Vernon collected stamps himself, he didn't keep this one because it was ugly. He sold it to a stamp dealer for a few shillings.

Vernon's ugly magenta stamp would gain notoriety and value through the years. Today it's valued at $500,000 to $750,000. It's not the most valuable stamp in the world—a Swedish stamp is priced at $3 million—but it's close.

Why is the one-cent British Guiana stamp so valuable? The primary reason is it's the only such stamp known to exist. However, it also has an interesting history.

British Guiana, now known as Guyana, lies on the northern coast of South America. Britain took it over as a sugar plantation colony in 1814. In 1856 the local postmaster ran out of stamps and asked the local newspaper to print a few to tide him over until a supply ship arrived.

Time was short, so the newspaper simply used the printing press block of a ship that usually ran above its shipping column. The newspaper also used its regular type face and a cheap magenta paper it had on hand. The stamps looked so primitive that postal officials signed or initialed each one so they couldn't be counterfeited easily.

Soon after the stamps were made, ships arrived with a fresh batch of stamps, and the one-cent British Guianas faded into oblivion until Vernon found the last one known to exist.

The background view shows the 741-feet-high Kaieteur Falls in Guyana.

HAWAII: MISSIONARY LETTERS

Stamps from "dead countries"—countries that no longer exist—are particularly collectable, and some collectors specialize in them. The earliest stamps from the Hawaiian islands are "dead country" stamps.

Before becoming part of the United States in 1900 and a full-fledged state in 1959, Hawaii was an independent string of volcanic islands in the middle of the Pacific Ocean. A king and queen ruled the island nation, gradually adopting Western practices such as the postal service. The island also welcomed Western missionaries, seeing religious education as a step toward entering modern life.

In 1851 Hawaiian leaders issued the country's first stamps. Because few native Hawaiians had use for the new system of communication and had very little need to communicate with the mainland, most of these first stamps were used by missionaries from the United States, who came to Hawaii to convert the Polynesians to Christianity in the mid-1800s. In fact, most of the stamps known to exist today came from letters mailed by missionaries to friends and family in America.

The simple no-frills stamps, in denominations of 2 cents, 5 cents, and 13 cents, were printed in Honolulu on Oahu with printing materials on hand. Because the 2-cent stamp, pictured here, was used to send local letters, it is the most rare. And "missionaries" of any denomination without damage are almost unknown.

The background view shows an outrigger canoe with sail in a Hawaiian lagoon.

LIBERIA: TOPSY-TURVY

An upside-down element in a stamp is a common printing error and one that nearly always increases its value. If collectors ever find a stamp with part of its design printed upside down, they will usually try to buy as many of these errors as possible and hold on to their finds.

The error occurs when a stamp is designed with two or more colors and has to go through the printing press at least two times. If the wrong end is put into the press during the second color printing, the second color's element will be upside down. It's an easy mistake to make.

The most famous example of an upside-down stamp is known as the "Jenny." It was printed in 1918 as the United States' first airmail stamp and depicted a flying plane. Only one sheet of 100 stamps was printed with the plane upside down, and these stamps are sought after and expensive.

Many other stamps, such as this elephant printed by Liberia in 1892, contain well-known upside-down errors. The elephant was the first of several Liberian stamp issues between 1892 and 1923 showing the wildlife of this country on the Atlantic coast of West Africa, bordered by Sierra Leone, Guinea, and the Ivory Coast.

This type of error has become more rare in recent years with computerized printing presses and quality control systems. But it's still possible to find a stamp that's printed upside down.

The background view shows grass houses along a sandy stretch of Liberia.

MAURITIUS: INVITED TO THE BALL

O n the little island of Mauritius in the Indian Ocean, plans for a lavish ball were underway. The island was one of many British colonies that produced sugarcane in 1847. Lady Gomm, whose husband, Sir Maynard Gomm, was the island's lieutenant general, wanted the ball to have an air of originality.

As Lady Gomm flipped through the mail that had recently arrived on a ship from England, she noticed that England's young Queen Victoria gazed out on the world from each tiny black stamp.

"That's it!" Lady Gomm exclaimed. The next day, Joseph Barnard, the local watchmaker, agreed to produce Mauritius's first stamp.

Barnard engraved two copies of the English stamps onto copper plates. He printed the one-penny stamp on dark orange paper and the two-penny on deep blue. On the right side, he printed "Mauritius" and on the left, "Post Office." He quickly printed 500 of each and rushed them to Lady Gomm. She loved these first stamps of the island and stuck one on each of her ball invitations. In all the excitement, no one noticed Barnard's error. The stamps should have read "Post Paid" rather than "Post Office."

As soon as those first 1,000 stamps were used up, Barnard printed a revised stamp with his error corrected. Because so few were produced, the first Mauritius stamps, often called "Post Offices," are rare and valuable. Only 26 are known to exist.

The background view shows an illustration of the extinct dodo bird. The Mauritius bird, which could not fly, was killed off by visiting sailors in 1681.

MEXICO: UNWELCOME EMPEROR

When the young Austrian Prince Maximilian and his bride Carlota arrived in Mexico in the spring of 1864, he expected to live a long time as the country's new emperor. Mexico had even printed stamps depicting Maximilian to celebrate their new leader.

But not everyone in Mexico was happy to have a foreigner ruling their country, especially a foreigner chosen by the French. A few years before, France had invaded Mexico because its new leader, Benito Juarez, had refused to pay Mexico's debt to several European countries, including France. But France had left Juarez alive, and that would cause problems for Maximilian.

Though Maximilian was a kind, harmless emperor, he wasn't a very astute leader. He failed to mollify the forces growing against him, particularly Juarez, who wanted to liberate his country from European influence.

By the summer of 1866 Juarez had taken control of several remote parts of Mexico. Many of the shipments of stamps bearing Maximilian's face were intercepted by Juarez's forces and destroyed. In June 1867 use of the stamps was abruptly stopped. Juarez had captured Mexico City, and Maximilian was on the run.

Just three years after assuming leadership, Maximilian was betrayed and captured while trying to flee Mexico. He was sentenced to death by firing squad. By 1879 after several years of confusion among postal officials, Juarez had stamps printed bearing his own likeness and cemented his leadership of the country.

NEW BRUNSWICK: PREENING POSTMASTER

efore 1859 Canada didn't make its own stamps or money but used ones made in Britain. But that year, Canada decided to replace the British currency with Canadian dollars. The decision meant Canada would now have to print its own stamps too. In the province of New Brunswick on Canada's eastern coast, the job fell to Postmaster General Charles Connell.

These first stamps were supposed to depict either Queen Victoria, the Prince of Wales, or a locomotive and steamship. Connell, however, had other ideas. He must have been a very self-confident man, sure of his own popularity and the respect of his community. He decided to replace the portrait of the prince with one of himself.

Well before the date the stamps were to be issued, Connell proudly showed the freshly printed stamps to other government officials. Instead of being pleased with their postmaster, Connell's colleagues were shocked at his unbelievable gall and ego. Connell had to resign under the outcry. The brown 5-cent stamps bearing his portrait were ordered destroyed.

A new green 5-cent stamp bearing Queen Victoria's portrait was ordered. But Connell and a few others managed to spirit away a few hundred of his vanity stamps. Since they were never officially issued or used, the stamps aren't considered proper postage stamps. But the story behind them has made Connell's stamps popular and valuable.

The background view shows a New Brunswick river, partially filled with logs. This maritime province lies directly north of Maine and used to supply large quantities of lumber.

NEWFOUNDLAND: CRASH MAIL

In 1919 Harry Hawker set out in a Sopwith plane to cross the Atlantic Ocean from Newfoundland to England. Hawker was trying to win a £10,000 prize offered by the *Daily Mail* newspaper for the first trans-Atlantic flight.

He didn't make it, crash landing in midocean. Fortunately for Hawker and his copilot, the Danish boat *Mary* happened to be nearby and picked them up. Another nearby ship was able to save the wrecked plane and the mailbag Hawker had been carrying. The background view shows an illustration of the landing and rescue.

Inside that mailbag were 200 letters bearing brown three-cent stamps depicting a caribou's head. Although many of these caribou stamps were printed, only 200 were overprinted with the words "First Trans-Atlantic Air Post April 1919" and signed on the back with J.A.R., the initials of J. A. Robinson, the postmaster of Newfoundland. The stamps had been marked specifically for this first airmail flight and sent with Hawker's plane.

Of the 200 stamped, airmail letters, all but 18 were retrieved from Hawker's wreck. For collectors, these stamps are not only rare but tell the amazing story of Canada's first attempt to deliver mail by air across the Atlantic and Hawker's crash and near-miraculous rescue.

Newfoundland, the most easterly Canadian province, issued several other special airmail stamps in small printings, but this first issue with its dramatic story remains the most rare and expensive.

NEW SOUTH WALES: WRONG VIEW

ew South Wales earned the title of the first Australian state to issue its own stamps, which were introduced on January 1, 1850. New South Wales lies on the southeastern coast of Australia and began as a British penal colony in 1788. This stamp is also special because it is one of the first picture stamps produced. Until then, stamps tended to show leaders of countries, coats of arms, or decorative designs rather than scenes from a country.

Although New South Wales' first stamps are known as "Sydney Views," the stamp probably doesn't depict Sydney Harbor. Instead it reproduces the colony's great seal, which shows convicts landing at Botany Bay with a few buildings visible in the background.

English convicts were transported by ship to Australia until 1852 as punishment for crimes and to populate the new colony. By the early 1800s, the colony had begun to export wool, and soon settlers were moving in among the convicts to herd sheep and sell wool. New South Wales had become an upstanding community, and in 1901 it joined with five other colonies to become the nation of Australia.

By 1851 the "Sydney Views" stamps were replaced by a series of stamps portraying Queen Victoria of England. Because of their distinction as the first Australian stamp and as one of the first pictorial stamps, and also because of the short duration of their issue, "Sydney Views" are rare.

The background view shows a famous modern view of Sydney Harbor Bridge, which was completed in 1931.

NICARAGUA: VOLCANIC POLITICS

Ever since Columbus sailed from Spain to the Americas looking for a route to the Far East, travelers and traders have sought a water route across North America or South America. By 1901 the United States had decided the isthmus of Central America would make an ideal place to carve out a canal and the long-hoped-for shortcut.

The United States was trying to decide whether to build the canal through Nicaragua or Panama. It looked as if Nicaragua would win the coveted canal, which would bring jobs and trade flooding into the poor country for the foreseeable future.

The U.S. Senate was in the midst of a final debate on the canal's location when each senator received this little stamp. It was delivered to them by a delegation from Panama in a last attempt to change the senators' minds and locate the canal in Panama.

Ironically, it was Nicaragua, which a year before had issued the stamp, that would bring the country's defeat in the bid for the canal. It portrayed the smoking volcano Momotombo in Nicaragua. When canal supporters in Panama came across the stamps, they knew they had a good chance of convincing American senators that Nicaragua, with all its supposed volcanic activity, was not a safe place for a canal.

They rushed the stamps to American senators, who quickly changed their minds and the canal's location before the Nicaraguans had a chance to defend their volcano.

The background view shows a ship in one of the Panama Canal locks.

RUSSIA: LAST CZAR

N o one could have guessed that five years after the first stamp bearing his image was issued, Russian Czar Nicholas II and his royal family would be shot to death by leaders of the Communist Revolution that swept through Russia in 1918. After Nicholas's death, the stamps became a memorial to this slain leader and the loss of Russia's czars and czarinas.

Postal officials in this huge land issued a set of 17 stamps showing portraits of czars for the first time in 1913 to celebrate the 300th anniversary of the Romanoff Dynasty. The dynasty officially began in 1613 but extended back to the 1300s, with Russian rulers consolidating their lands and calling themselves czars.

Many of Russia's notable czars and czarinas—along with views of the Kremlin, the Winter Palace, and the Romanoff Palace—were immortalized in the series. The two czars shown here are Nicholas II and Peter the Great, who introduced European culture to Russia and moved the capital from Moscow to St. Petersburg.

The stamps were unpopular, however, with two groups. Church leaders thought they were sacrilegious because the czar also acted as the head of Russia's church. Defiling a czar's likeness with a postmark defiled the church, they thought. Russian peasants also balked at seeing the face of their "Little Father's" face marred by the heavy postmark. At first the stamps didn't sell well because of the outcry, but after several months the fervor died down and stamp sales picked up.

Today the stamps aren't valuable, but they recount Russia's long dynasty of czars and czarinas.

SERBIA: DEATH MASK

hen King Peter I came to the Serbian throne in 1904, postal officials decided to mark his coronation with a commemorative stamp. Because the coronation also fell on the 100-year anniversary of Peter's ruling dynasty, the stamp celebrated both the coronation and the anniversary.

The design showed Peter's profile alongside the profile of the founder of Peter's dynasty, Karageorge. Eager to get the new stamp to the people, officials had a French engraver make the printing plates.

Shortly after the stamps were released, however, they realized the stamp showed more than Peter and his ancestor. When the stamp was turned upside down, a grizzly death mask appeared over the faces of the two leaders. People believed the grinning mask showed King Alexander I, Peter's predecessor, who had been assassinated in 1903. The stamp on the right shows the death mask outlined in white.

The French engraver insisted he knew nothing about the mask. But he quickly fled when questioned, and many people believed he intentionally created the death mask for someone who wanted revenge against Alexander's murder.

Alexander's mother, the Queen Mother Natalie, seemed the prime suspect. The truth remains a mystery even today. After World War I, the Serbs united with Croats and Slovenes to create Yugoslavia, which today has broken apart into its former states amidst much bloodshed.

Although the stamps are worth only a few dollars, counterfeit copies pop up now and then. Most likely, the fake stamps were made to defraud the postal system in the years after the original issue, rather than to fool collectors.

SICILY: FRAMED

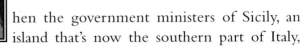

When the government ministers of Sicily, an island that's now the southern part of Italy, decided to issue the country's first stamp in 1858, they were careful to pick just the right design to launch their modern postal system. After a short debate, the ministers agreed that the "sacred effigy" of their king was the most appropriate design.

They knew King Ferdinand II—whose nickname was Bomba—would like the idea. However, they also knew he would *not* like the idea of his "sacred effigy" being marred by a postmark like other countries used, which left a circle of ink across the stamp. The ministers knew that some kind of postmark was necessary. The postmark told postal officials that a stamp had been used and prevented people from cheating the postal system by using the same stamps again and again.

The ministers thought long and hard. How could they honor King Ferdinand with a stamp in his likeness yet prevent that likeness from being marked up?

The solution they came up with was simple yet elegant. They designed a postmark in the shape of a frame. A frame would let postal officials know when a stamp had been used, and the king's "sacred effigy" would be highlighted, rather than obliterated, by the postmark.

Only two years after the stamp was issued an insurrection began in Sicily as people fought to oust Ferdinand and unite with Italy. A year later, Sicily did become part of Italy.

The background view shows the Temple of Concord at Girgenti in Sicily.

SPAIN: WHOOPS

Some stamps are so rare or strange that everyone assumes they're fakes—until proof of their authenticity turns up, if it ever does. In this case, a simple little error was made while printing a simple little stamp in 1851.

Spain's postal authorities decided to make a plain blue stamp showing Queen Isabella II's portrait. The stamp sold for six reals, the Spanish equivalent of cents. To print big sheets of the stamps, printers made clichés, or metal casts of the stamp design, and rolled them across the printing plate to create multiple impressions of the design.

In this case, a printer accidentally included a cliché from a different stamp issue, a two-real stamp. The result on each sheet was dozens of six-real stamps with one two-real stamp mixed in by accident.

Because the two-real stamp was usually red, this one, mistakenly colored blue, stood out. Experts decided the blue two-real stamp was a forgery and dismissed it. But between 1922 and 1925 the famous stamp collection of Count Philippe von Ferrari was opened for inspection. Inside the pages, a pair of stamps showing the six-real and the two-real still joined together was found. That proved the authenticity to most experts.

It's estimated that 145 blue two-real stamps once existed, but only three have surfaced. Today the rare error is valued at $110,000.

The background view shows the sprawling, 18th-century Renaissance Royal Palace in Madrid, the capital of this southern European country on the Atlantic Ocean.

SPORTS ON DISPLAY

ports stamps are some of the most popular for collectors who specialize in topical collecting. Greece issued the first sports stamp in 1896, the year the first modern Olympic Games were held in Athens. Greece created a series of 12 stamps showing scenes from the ancient Olympics once held there.

In the past 100 years, more countries have issued more stamps commemorating the Olympic Games than all other sports stamps combined. Even countries that didn't participate in the games have issued Olympic stamps. Here, two Olympic stamps are shown: a runner issued by Holland to commemorate the 1928 Games and a bobsled issued by Germany to commemorate the 1936 Games.

Of course, other sporting competitions often earn commemorative stamps, such as the one pictured here of a soccer player issued by Italy for the World Cup games in 1934. In recent years it's become popular to issue stamps honoring particular sports rather than competitions.

It's hard to name a sport that hasn't been pictured on a stamp. In fact, with the growing popularity of sports, postal officials have issued stamps showing new or more off-beat sports such as skin diving, judo, water skiing, parachuting, and golf. Sports heroes on stamps are also becoming increasingly popular.

In countries where a particular sport is popular, a continuous series of stamps depicting that sport is often issued. In China Ping-Pong stamps are most popular, while in Eastern Europe bicycling stamps are all the rage.

STAMPS IN ODD SHAPES

Most stamps are square or rectangular, but some collectors specialize in stamps with unusual shapes. A few countries, such as Colombia, have even developed a penchant for issuing stamps in odd shapes.

Colombia issued one of the world's first triangular stamps in 1865. The design contained three views of the country's coat of arms, each set at a different angle so that no matter which way you turned the stamp, one of the coats of arms appeared right side up. Colombia issued another triangular stamp four years later.

Countries issue stamps in odd shapes for two reasons: first, for use as a stamp for parcels or letters handled in a special way—airmail for example; second, to attract collectors, although stamp societies generally frown on issues printed specifically to lure collectors.

In 1898, when the Turks invaded and occupied the Greek province of Thessaly, a series of five stamps, one of which is shown here, was issued from the country. All five stamps were eight-sided, or octagonal, and these were the first stamps of this shape produced.

Other odd-shaped stamps include this diamond-shaped parcel stamp from Salvador. Circular stamps have been issued by Afghanistan, British Guiana, and Kashmir, among other countries. The Tonga Islands in the Pacific Ocean surprised the world by issuing stamps resembling gold coins and printed on gold foil. Sierra Leone issued stamps shaped like its national borders.

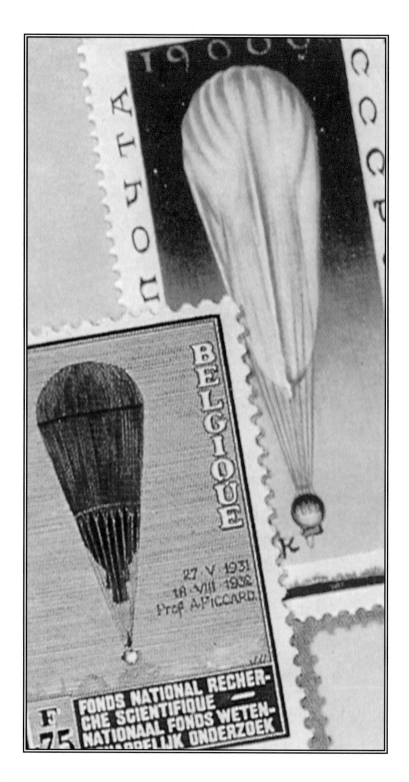

STRATOSPHERIC FLIGHTS

hen Professor Auguste Piccard sailed a hot-air balloon far into the stratosphere, or upper layer of the atmosphere, his fellow Belgium citizens were so proud that they created a stamp to commemorate his two flights in 1931 and 1932. The 1932 issue was more than a way to show the country's pride; it also helped raise money for Piccard's scientific investigations into the temperatures and composition of the upper atmosphere.

The next year, Russian aeronauts topped Piccard's stratospheric flight by sailing 19,000 feet into the atmosphere on September 30. Russia quickly issued stamps commemorating the record-breaking flight. To emphasize the height the new balloon reached, the stamp was tall and showed a bit of the Moscow skyline at the base.

Neither stamp is worth a great deal, ranging from $21 to $100 for a complete set, which includes three stamps each. But for collectors who are drawn to topical collecting of the human quest for high flight and space exploration, these stamps represent some of the first attempts to reach beyond Earth. They also show the pride and determination many countries felt as they pushed to the edges of their knowledge and beyond.

These and later investigations into the layer of atmosphere 10 to 30 miles above Earth's surface led scientists to discover that most of the atmospheric ozone, which protects the Earth's surface from harmful ultraviolet rays, lies in the lower stratosphere.

UNITED STATES: PRE-STAMP STAMPS

he U.S. Congress didn't approve a uniform postal rate using prepaid stamps until five years after Great Britain came up with the idea. But that didn't stop private postal services from organizing and issuing their own stamps. In 1842 several such companies adopted systems similar to Britain's to make sending letters in America easier and less expensive.

By 1845 the U.S. Congress realized England's postal system, along with these private services, was working wonders. Congress passed a law that created a similar postal system. However, they failed to give any particular person or governmental department the authority to print and issue stamps. The United States had a new postal system but no stamps to put it in motion.

Fortunately, local postmasters used their own initiative to solve the problem. The postmaster in New York was the first to issue his own stamp. Others soon followed, creating stamps known as "provisionals" for the new postal system.

One of the best-known provisional stamps was created by David Bryan, the postmaster of Alexandria, Virginia. Bryan issued the distinctive circular stamp in 1846. Only a few copies of Bryan's stamp exist today, and they are quite valuable.

By 1847 Congress corrected its oversight and gave stamp printing and issuing authority to the Postmaster General of the United States. The need for local provisional stamps like Bryan's was gone.

The background view shows the historic Alexandria Christ Church in which President George Washington and Northern Civil War General Robert E. Lee worshipped.

VIRGIN ISLANDS: MISSING VIRGIN

It's hard to believe, but this stamp is worth $75,000 simply because someone made a mistake when printing it. Stamp issues from the Virgin Islands in the mid-1800s often portrayed either the Virgin Mary or Saint Ursula in the center, with decorative borders. In an 1867–1868 issue, however, the Virgin didn't make it to her place of honor on a few stamps.

The stamp featured a crimson background with the Virgin in black. But an error was made while the stamps were being printed, and on a few of the stamps a blaze of white, rather than the Virgin, marks the center.

Such missing-color errors are relatively common. They occur only in stamps with two or more colors, and it happens when one color doesn't make it onto the stamp. Sometimes a printer will just forget to add the second color. Other times, two pages are stuck together during the second-color printing so that the second color only gets printed on the top page.

In the case of the missing Virgin, a few stamps didn't make it through the black printing press. Experts suspect that the missing Virgin stamps were likely part of a printer's trial run that wasn't meant to be sold. The real error happened when the stamps weren't thrown in the garbage.

There are eight known copies of the missing Virgin. They have become valuable because of their rarity and the religious nature of the error.

The background view shows a beach leading out to sea from one of the Virgin Islands, which include a hundred small islands in the Caribbean Sea.

CHRONOLOGY

4000 B.C.   The first known postal service began in China, when rulers dispatched runners with messages and orders.

550–629 B.C.   King Kyros II of Persia established the earliest well-regulated message service using horses and riders waiting at relay stations along designated routes.

A.D. 105   In China, Ts'ai Lun invented paper, which spread throughout Europe to replace messages written on stone, wood, wax, and animal skins.

1200   The word "post" in the modern meaning was first used by Pope Honorius III.

1300   The first paper mills were established in Europe.

1505   The first private postal service, available to anyone who could pay for delivery, was created by an Italian nobleman, Francesco de Tassis, in Austria.

1661   Henry Bishop introduced the first postmark in England.

1840   Sir Rowland Hill invented the adhesive, prepaid postage stamp in Great Britain.

1841   A young girl wrote a letter in a British newspaper, asking readers to send her postage stamps, becoming the first known stamp collector.

1847 The United States, following Britain's example, issued its first modern stamp.

1856 The first philatelic club, The Omnibus Club, was founded in the United States.

1862 The first stamp album was printed.

1863 The first stamp catalog was published.

1874 The Universal Postal Union was established to regulate mail from different countries and fix universal postage rates.

1918 The first stamp specifically designed to carry air-mail, the "Jenny," was issued.

1926 The first international philatelist organization, the International Federation of Philately, was created.

INDEX ❧

FURTHER READING

Bierman, Stanley. *World's Greatest Stamp Collectors*. Sidney, Ohio: Linns Stamp News, 1990.

Burns, Peggy. *The Mail (Stepping Through History)*. New York: Thomson Learning, 1995.

Datz, Stephen R. *Catalogue of Errors on U.S. Postage Stamps (1996/97)*. Iola, Wis.: Krause Publications, 1997.

Datz, Stephen R. *Collecting Stamps (Instant Expert)*. Brooklyn, NY: Alliance Publishing, 1996.

Griffenhagen, George, and Husak, Jerome. *Adventures in Topical Stamp Collecting*. Second edition. Milwaukee: American Topical Association, 1981.

Sharpe, William F. *Linn's Guide to Stamp Collecting Software and Collecting on the Internet*. Sidney, Ohio: Linns Stamp News, 1997.